THE MIND'S ILLUSIONS

THE MIND'S ILLUSIONS

SERAPHINA BLAKE

CONTENTS

1 The Roots of Misguided Thoughts   1
2 Introduction to the Nature of Illusions   5
3 The Cycle of Suffering   9
4 Tools for Breaking the Illusion   11
5 Cultivating Mindfulness and Awareness   15
6 The Role of Compassion in Ending Suffering   17
7 Case Studies and Real-Life Examples   21
8 Conclusion: Embracing Clarity and Wisdom   25

Copyright © 2024 by Seraphina Blake
All rights reserved. No part of this book may be reproduced in any manner whatsoever without written permission except in the case of brief quotations embodied in critical articles and reviews.
First Printing, 2024

CHAPTER 1

The Roots of Misguided Thoughts

The world we experience is born from our misguided thoughts. These misguided thoughts may stem from appetites that are blinded by raw desire, dukkhaṭṭha - contexts of suffering. Dukkhaṭṭha may obscure the destructive results of our behaviors leading to situations in which people believe that torture, sexual violence, and theft are virtuous. The results of dukkhaṭṭha may lead to potentially dangerous delusions regarding the complexity of our world.

Cognitive bias can skew our perception to the point of creating illusions, such that factors that support our preferred ideas are strongly noticed while factors contradicting our preferred ideas are either strongly downplayed or are not even noticed. The philosopher and mathematician René Descartes believed that the power to amp up the intensity of certain sensory experiences was the work of the Devil. This was the face of a moral illusion. Descartes was mistaken in the sense that the phenomena he was experiencing was not being tampered with, it was simply enriched with mental influence.

The psychological illusion, created and reinforced suggests two explanations for this effect: Priming and the peak-end rule. Firstly, hearing disquieting music which suggests danger, suggests danger. Secondly, the confetti which repeatedly hits the back of a head that is waiting to experience a frightening event, indicates a likely major event. The final aspect of the deception is linked to the concept of psychic numbing. It would seem counterintuitive or even nonsensical that most decent people, those that possess empathy and are good-hearted, would get bored of, ignore, or dismiss mass suffering. And yet today millions of people eat, sleep, and work each day while prospering from investments in companies using near-slave child labor. They barely bat an eye regarding how severe is the resulting abuse and death. Could there be anything they might learn from their apathy and mass-murderous complicity?

Cognitive Biases and Their Impact on Perception
What are cognitive biases and how do they affect our perception? Our perception of the world is, in a word, biased. Our thoughts are shaped and distorted by the beliefs and perspectives we have accumulated in the past, and through time they become unable to see reality clearly and with the whole scope it presents. We can observe this in the human thought process, which is strictly associated with our experience. We can know about things like the color, texture, or temperature of objects we have an intimate connection with. However, we can learn through research and investigation about other things that range only a little beyond our daily experiences. This is because the data available to our senses can be constricted or enhanced, depending on special conditions. Our thoughts, whose objects of thought are clearly related to the data developed through its development, then turn into concepts and so become constricted and limited.

This is, of course, natural and expected, but if we do not connect with things on the basis of the data available to us now, then our thoughts become illusions and are disconnected from reality. The way we believe the world is like creates our behavior. Illusions are, in short, the thoughts that affect us and our actions.

CHAPTER 2

Introduction to the Nature of Illusions

Illusions are statements, images, or experiential events that are in some way off-kilter. In art, for example, one image or painting can represent two very different items. An image can appear to be a young woman with her head turned or an old woman with her eyes closed depending on the mental resolve and the choice to attend to one or the other features of the perceptual experience. In other cases, illusions occur at direct levels of experience, such as in the case of dreams or hallucinations. Much of the time, such errors in perception or conception are entertaining and a focus of attention.

Illusions that come by way of distortive experiences, thoughts, or emotional states often pass quickly into oblivion, if not to some form of pride or slight embarrassment with respect to normal functioning. Still, in their extreme forms, illusions can become the very seat of delusional thought, extreme suffering, and psychiatric disorder. This occurs when delusional thinking traps people into a morass of content whereby they come to believe something that is not true and move in a pattern of thought or logic based on an ill-constructed schema or activity.

The thoughts that create extreme illusions of truth and activity may operate at more primitive levels regarding the loss of perceptual or conceptual grounding in ways that give rise to the distressing aspect of suffering. In contrast to the 'truth' of thinking that gives logic to our everyday discourse and experience, there are thoughts of a different order. These thoughts arise in the mind and possess a distorting effect that may pull one into negative emotional states that seem, in some sense, as more 'real' than do ordinary thoughts.

There is a tendency to categorize thoughts as 'good' and 'bad' on the basis of their content and eventual effects and to keep track of them in terms of 'how much' we suffer or do not suffer on the basis of their initiation. The content of thought is described, in any number of psychotherapy paradigms, as 'automatic thoughts' that keep one locked into patterns of behavior and belief that are not only unlikely in fact to be true but also maintain or exacerbate a disposition to suffering in various mental disorders, such as panic disorder, obsessive-compulsive disorder, and depression. The method of thought, the so-called heuristics or guide points by which we move through experience, is rarely emphasized.

Given that experience is guided in a most self-referential manner through concepts—be they ideas about how the external world works, such as mechanical laws, or how we are to interact with others—any misaligned thought will necessarily misalign experience. These thoughts can be branded as illusions: perfectly natural, albeit distorted, events based on the now-misguided heuristics of everyday thought.

Defining Illusions in the Context of the Mind

For the sake of our discussion, I will use the term "illusions" to denote mistaken or distorted conception of a belief or object—i.e., a conception that does not match reality. While the idea of "mind's illusions" denotes false beliefs or impressions, it also refers to (emotional) ignorance; true knowledge about an object enables one to regulate their aversions or affections toward that object, and to act smoothly, while an ignorance arising from illusions creates ignorance about the proper object of affection or aversion, and therefore keeps one ensnared in extremes. In a more general or neutral fashion, we might also use the idea of illusions to discuss any belief that does not cohere with reality in general. Frequently, illusions arise from diareta (in the broadest sense, "thoughts" of any kind), and are dependent upon and maintain habitual tendencies.

Such illusions generate significant amounts of suffering—that is their main short-term damage. In the long-term, and when left unchecked, they further lead to the perpetuation of suffering. By generation of suffering, I also mean possibility for generation: illusions have a "projective" nature, causing one to act in ways that will bring suffering. However, if we simply consider our life, we can fully recognize the perceptible degree of suffering created by our own illusions of the mind: when we have something we dislike due to our ignorance, we often respond to it by pushing it away, when we desire something we feel that we are not managing we respond by clinging and further amplifying the suffering, and when something we like ends, we experience dissatisfaction.

CHAPTER 3

The Cycle of Suffering

Misguided thinking in itself generates suffering. Misguided thinking takes the form of what the Buddhist tradition calls the three poisons: anger, desire (clinging), and ignorance. When thinking is penetrated by the poisons, it becomes the lens through which we see everything. Although we attempt to manipulate the world so things will satisfy or calm us, that manipulation is an impossible goal since the troubles are produced by our own minds. Trying to manipulate others leads to even more difficulty.

The cycle begins with an illusion about the world or ourselves. This illusion generates a mismatch between our experience and the idealized experience we have emboldened from our thoughts. The result is suffering, which leads to a need for change. This act of change manifests in many forms. Most often we take out our frustrations on those closest to us. We become irritable, argumentative, or silent. Alternatively, we blame whatever we think caused the pain in the first place, which may include individuals, circumstances, the self, or the world at large. Schlesinger reveals a central dynamic here, which is immediately recognizable in a world at war. When things do not match our ideals, we seldom consider the beliefs that generate those ideals. Instead, we focus on changing the people, things, or circumstances we believe are responsible for our suffering. Rather than examining our thoughts, we attempt to force the world to correspond to our thoughts about it. This looks different at a larger scale, but the mechanism can easily be recognized.

Identifying Patterns of Misguided Thinking

We now come to the practical part of the book. This is where we start to identify the patterns of misguided thinking that sweater the world of the mind. It is crucial to do this. It is crucial because as long as we live blindly at the mercy of every thought that pushes our buttons and only serves to ladle out more suffering and sculpt one brain pattern after another, we shall continue to be their victims. The following faulty patterns of subjective experience are arranged roughly in the order of the sheer level of belief that they tend to breed.

When explaining these, you will see that the mind's illusions and its raw, deluded thoughts dovetail very interestingly with those presented in the Shurangama sutra. Let us therefore address each pattern as a way to work with thoughts. No one is doomed to suffer. Everyone who has ever hated someone knows what self-hatred is like. And after hating oneself for some time, there can be an upsurge of rebellion against oneself for allowing the self-hatred. But as we take a stand against hating ourselves, and are revolted by that self-hatred, we feed the very self-hatred we are trying to stop. In any one of these twisted cases, using reason alone will not pull us out of the sickly web of personal loathing. To stop seeing oneself as fundamentally unlovable, it is essential to see how the mind creates a reality of someone who is unworthy of love. The following advice is offered for all thoughts in the sections below.

CHAPTER 4

Tools for Breaking the Illusion

The Mind's Illusions
Cognitive restructuring, a central technique in CBT, is about countering, questioning, and breaking down irrational or unhelpful cognitions that we might be holding. It allows us to loosen these false or distressing beliefs and break through them by way of reason and other techniques. It's designed to increase mental wellbeing, thought clarity, and coping. Techniques vary, but at the centre of them all is the act of speaking back or thinking back against the mistaken and misguided thoughts that are causing us difficulty. Moreover, these techniques offer a means of change that can tackle a host of different distressing cognitions and thereby unlock peace of mind so that there is less compulsion toward the paths that suffering takes. That is, we can gain insight and clarity through these techniques, regardless of the particular forms of false views that are causing us trouble.

Mindfulness is a big part of many different schools of psychotherapy and spiritual practice. In a simplified sense, it has something in common with diffusion techniques in CBT. It's about being present in our minds, observing and experiencing whatever comes up, without getting lost, dominated, or framed by the details. Meditation in this style focuses attention on the here and now, so that we can "step back" and watch the passions and thoughts go by, without becoming swept away and believing them to be an accurate commentary on reality. The practice involves a disciplined observation of one's thoughts, or potentially physical sensations such as breathing or the feeling of eating. In various ways, it embodies the idea of watching various thoughts and feelings pass us by – same idea, very different technique.

Cognitive Behavioral Techniques

Some of the techniques that have been used to challenge illusions at the level of conscious will are pulled from the growing list of cognitive behavioral techniques. Gene Parr codified a number of them in a self-help format. These techniques systematically challenge all the facets of each of the cognitive illusions that we studied. Parr and others have found that these methods work: they give at least temporary relief from the impact of the illusions. This evidence is important in that it supports the idea that limbering up some of the generally malnourished resources of the conscious will is helpful in bringing about relief from misery. So what are these techniques? In the remainder of this section, we offer a selection; they are presented in no particular order but rather are arranged to offer the reader a taste of the possible tools to challenge illusions.

1. Talk back: Discuss the issues with a good friend. It's important to take a perspective on your thoughts and discuss whether they are actually realistic or based on reality. Use logic to answer some of your own beliefs (for example, the belief that one mistake will ruin your project or career) and explain to your friend why they don't make sense.

2. Dr. Jekyll and Mr. Hyde: First, split off and make a note of two parts of yourself: Your Dr. Jekyll side (the positive, healthy and fun side) and your Mr. Hyde side (the demanding, downbeat, stressed side). Describe those two sides of yourself. Try to treat yourself with a little respect and concern by finding some evidence of the existence of your Dr. Jekyll side. What evidence is there of a better Dr. Jekyll side to you?

CHAPTER 5

Cultivating Mindfulness and Awareness

Meditative practice is a method for cultivating clarity and mindfulness. Its subjective essence is about moving from being identified with the foreground of, to assuming the position of witness to, what unfolds at any particular moment in the field of consciousness. Whenever our thoughts, emotions, and outer world preoccupy us, our concentration is absorbed in a thin layer of the totality of experience. This is the illusory trance of surface things, and our suffering's roots are embedded here.

And in a way, it is arbitrary, since we are accustomed to being here. Hypnosis. Mindfulness and awareness are the perspectives that promote a clearer perception. They aim to create a "radical" shift in consciousness, extending from the mental trance of surface experience to an awareness advertising deconditioned field of movement, personal space, thoughts and other phenomena. Careful attention may be focused more on time-intensive mindfulness exercises that help in recognizing mind-states. Alternatively, attentional exercises leading to improved flow and energy state, along with therapy directed at uncovering the unconscious by studying the split between obliviousness and what we care to know, may prove of benefit.

While the "assignment" posed by hypnotic suggestions is that of increased suggestibility and self-knowledge (i.e. awareness through suggestion), the aim of meditative inquiry is always to deepen understanding of the self and world.

Practices for Developing a Clearer Perception
Mind can alter reality due to its complex perception of the environment. This can be compared to the well-known optical illusion in which two lines appear to be of different lengths when placed atop an assortment of lines; while variations in length are visible to the eye, the mind interprets the context incorrectly. The brain, likewise, might project both the negative and the positive outcomes, leading to one's anxiety regarding the future.

Practices for developing a clearer perception

The value of these more general approaches is that they help one develop the ability to clearly see what is happening around oneself. It is this ability, which is sometimes referred to as "mindfulness" or "awareness," that provides the very faculties for perceiving the nature of the mind, misguided thoughts, connected mental events, and ultimately the nature of existence. It is these kinds of meditative techniques, which work with the basics of developing a clear and precise faculty of mental perception, that can constitute both the beginning of the path to profound transformation and a lifeline for those caught in the grip of suicidal thoughts. These are not supplements, to be tacked onto a larger course of medication or talk therapy. They are not always easy techniques. Rather, they are the real deal, and the foundation for the comprehensive practices of developing the happiness and mental stability that go beyond, precede, and prevent the more extreme forms of our mental muddles.

CHAPTER 6

The Role of Compassion in Ending Suffering

A simple awareness of the mechanisms our mind uses to create and end suffering does not lead to a reduction in it. To end the suffering created by misguided thoughts, we need to apply an appropriate antidote, a direct experiential counter, a personal lived experience that is the polar opposite of the experience created by the misguided ('afflictive') thought. There are many types of misguided thoughts and as a result, many possible antidotes. Of these, the ultimate, most powerful, and universal antidote is compassion. Compassion is the essence of the ancient Indian/Wisdom traditions. It is central to most of the major religions such as Christianity, Buddhism, Hinduism, Taoism, Islam, and Judaism and is emphasized in evolutionary psychology, philosophy, and sociology. While the doctrines and understandings vary, what is common to all these systems is the recognition that compassion has a genuine mental healing capacity. When one genuinely feels it, thinks it, and acts it, one's mental state is transformed. When genuinely felt, compassion has a transformative effect on our outlook on life, relationships, and the world around us.

It is not only ancient wisdom that places a high value on compassion. So too does modern psychology. Empathic concern, which is another word for compassion, is a key part of Altruism Research. Researchers have placed a very high value on the study of compassion and have come to the conclusion that this 'welling up of the heart' is amongst the most powerful and personal spinal solutions to the suffering that plagues our minds. Indeed, modern research has found that helping others can reduce mortality and reduce the impact of stress.

Empathy and its Healing Power

Empathy is complete identification with another: I may see that I, too, could suffer as you do, and your suffering becomes my own. Compassion then takes this feeling of universal connectedness and adds the desire that it change for the better. John Kabat-Zinn of the University of Massachusetts Medical School's Stress Reduction Clinic compares the human willed capacity to show empathy and compassion to a laid thermostat that aims to maintain a halfway, hence delivering a potential autonomic healing effect. Both of these prosocial tendencies are also expressions of illusions, in that they are based on the belief that what is happening should not be happening other than ideologically and scientifically shown. If the exhibited empathy has an explicit agenda, it will be projected from a sense of one's own wound connectedness: the empathizing believes themselves to have the solution for that which they identify as the pathology of the empathized, without adequately considering the other person's suffering, beliefs, and resources.

Empathizing, feeling compassion as empathy, and making a compassionate act that in itself reflects the perception of the patient's subjective qualities, beliefs, and resources, and which elicits real hope, is perceived by recipients as helping. This can have a profound healing effect. Compassion should be directed against suffering caused by illusions, notes the Dalai Lama, such as the overvaluation of items, the self-concept, or any of the others mentioned above that may result in a degradation of those who lack such connections or are not perceived to have them. The greatest form of compassion is hope, according to Dr. Viktor Frankl. The therapist must look for a glimmer of this and respond thereto shrewdly. The most relentless victim that I have suggested to be therapeutic to others in order to reduce his or her own suffering triggered by sustaining illusions is to a considerable extent alleviated. In the same way, the therapist may feel less lonely and isolated, decrease professional degeneracy, and alleviate personal prejudices and pain.

CHAPTER 7

Case Studies and Real-Life Examples

Case study I: Jill. A 26-year-old woman who spent years accumulating high grades and dreaming of success in a medical career developed paralyzing anxiety with panic attacks related to studying and to future evaluations. She believed she couldn't stand it if she did not attain her goals, or if she succeeded but lost what she accomplished. In treatment, she gradually realized that although she felt trapped in a double bind, the underlying logic was flawed and she developed self-compassion. She allowed herself to be sad and anxious about the possibility of a life other than she had hoped for and worked with her fear of failing, which she had suppressed for years. She eventually chose not to try to get into medical school. Many windows are left unopened, but points of view make them seem open and closed. Illusion is what drives our misconceptions and makes us feel trapped. This guide includes numerous case studies and examples of actual people who ended illusions and clarified priorities and overall aims.

Alisa. Certified as a nurse 12 years earlier and property manager at a medical practice, Alisa finished raising her daughters and felt she was in a tremendous rut. "Maybe there is really nothing fundamentally wrong with my life, but I feel oppressed," she said. She decided to leave medical practice and return to college to get an art history degree, but was not sure how to afford college tuition. I don't blame myself for being in a rut, but I don't seem able to escape. I feel trapped sometimes by the thought that if I try to change my circumstances, I'll be found to be really foolish, and so my present is "good enough" right now. The illusion, she later realized, was the idea that she couldn't escape her trap. She is now enjoying school, works with other people she likes, and likes feeling free from the notorious "cancer connection" that connects her work to the everyday stresses of illness and pain.

Illustrative Stories of Overcoming Illusions

David is experiencing a low mood and believes he's failing in life. He is having thoughts such as "I'm not living up to my potential" and "I'm inadequate." In addition to being emotionally painful, these thoughts are likely to increase and perpetuate the low mood he is experiencing. In the coming chapters, we'll offer strategies to help David deal with these thoughts so that they have less impact on his life.

Teshana is 30 years old and feels that her low mood is a result of a stressful period in her life. Teshana's parents compared her to her male cousins throughout her childhood, and her siblings unintentionally do the same thing now that they're adults. They say things like, "How come you haven't reached x milestone, but John has?" Teshana is aware of the fact that it's silly to compare herself to others, and she knows she doesn't need to reach expectations set by others. But the thoughts around this issue keep popping up. As a result, Teshana often feels like she is worthless since she has yet to achieve her goals. However, instead of wallowing in her low mood, Teshana often sets herself small achievable goals each week. Although she often considers not completing them (since they are so small), Teshana does so and feels proud when she does. Each goal she accomplishes helps her to prove to herself that she is not worthless. Even though doing so can be difficult, Teshana sometimes also has work done around the house to prove to herself that she is not lazy. By reminding herself that she doesn't need to fit into a mold created by others and instead setting herself small achievable tasks while remembering that she's only human, Teshana is living a life on autopilot.

CHAPTER 8

Conclusion: Embracing Clarity and Wisdom

Illusions, in any other context, would generally involve a magician or someone trying to pull the wool over our eyes. Yet, as we have discovered, the mind's illusions powerfully sap the mind of peace and contentment. When we act on our illusions, our suffering, as well as the suffering of those around us, perpetuates and grows. False thoughts of I, false thoughts of you, and false thoughts of attachment can be either guides to endless suffering or events on the path to boundless joy. When we are unnecessarily confused by our thoughts, we can succinctly see how they lead to pain. Going against our nature by focusing only on ourselves, distorting our reality, or ignoring reality leads to conflict at many levels. Furthermore, when these thought processes dominate our mind, we go against our natural empathetic origin, lose touch with it and cultivate its complete opposite, making our overriding thoughts of self-centeredness and care only for ourselves.

At the heart of the Buddhist teaching are mean and vast, compassion and wisdom, skillful and unskillful, illusions and correct. When our mistaken thoughts of view, attachment and distorted compassion grow, then our heart and source of happiness are blocked. What is therefore necessary is to combine the understanding of what to stop (mistaken ways of seeing, the ways we are attached to inappropriate objects, the feelings of aversion, and neutral attitudes), the inappropriate ways we then engage in speech, action, effort, concentration, mind and understanding so that we can transform our vision of wisdom to see that which really makes us happy, and our mountainous love and compassion into realizations of how we can help solve the immediate and far-going suffering of ourselves and those we can benefit. If we wish to be able to help more directly, then we have to study the correct way to live so that we can directly embody the knowledge of when to hold and when to let go, and move between thinking and not thinking.

www.ingramcontent.com/pod-product-compliance
Lightning Source LLC
LaVergne TN
LVHW092102060526
838201LV00047B/1535